D1173711

Canaletto

On cover
Canal Grande Looking Northeast, from Palazzo
Balbi to the Rialto Bridge, *detail, ca. 1719–23.*
Venice, Ca' Rezzonico.

Texts by Alberto Cottino
Translation by Jeffrey Jennings

Photograph credits
Sergio Anelli, Milan
Electa Archive, Milan
Banca Nazionale del Lavoro Archive, Rome
Osvaldo Böhm, Venice
Christie's, Rome
Giorgio Nimatallah/Luisa Ricciarini, Milan
Scala, Florence
Fine Arts and Monuments Registry, Parma

© 1996 by **Electa**, Milan
Elemond Editori Associati
All rights reserved

Printed for Electa
by the Stabilimento di Martellago (Venice)

Canaletto

Electa/Art Books International

Antonius Canale..
Origine Civis
Venetus

Canaletto

With the advent of the 18th century, the historical, social and cultural panorama of Europe was undergoing a profound transformation. The absolute power of the French sovereign Louis XIV was at its height; that of the Spanish king was practically exhausted. Meanwhile in England, France, Germany, the Low Countries and, at least in part, also in Italy, there began to take hold a new current of thought which would increasingly come to define the era, becoming thoroughly internationalized in the process. This current, known as the Enlightenment, sounded a call to the light of reason, to philosophy and science, profoundly influencing society by leading it gradually toward a radical restructuring of moral and ethical values among the bourgeois laity and, in England, toward the first phase of an industrial and technological revolution. Art was not left unaffected by these new tendencies. The first half of the 18th century saw the demise of the glorious baroque and Rococo periods, in which Italian artists had played such an important role (it is no coincidence that the last great baroque artist was an Italian, Giovanni Battista Tiepolo), and the opening of a transitional period, rife with contradictions, which would usher into the second half of the century the phenomenon of neoclassicism, an attempt to recuperate in a rationalistic way the objectivity of the Greco-Roman tradition; an attempt that was in fact rather short-lived, soon to be displaced in the opening years of the next century by the overt subjectivity of Romanticism.

The genre known as "veduta painting" (from the Italian word for "view"), heir to the great landscape tradition of the Netherlands, was born of the desire to

Giovan Battista Piazzetta, *Portrait of Canaletto*, engraving.

rationalize and simplify the idealized Classical landscapes of the 17th century, and as such tended to prefer the representation of real and recognizable places, and to prioritize the value of image over meaning. In this one recognizes a correlation, also in Italy, between the new genre and new bourgeois values of the Enlightenment. Indeed, veduta painting was an exclusively commercial phenomenon (except in the case of the "courtier," Bernardo Bellotto), exempt from the problematics of Classical or religious culture, and immediately comprehensible to everyone. The diffusion in England of Venetian vedutas, with their horizontal format and medium dimensions—"parlour-size," one could well say—suggests a sort of protocapitalist collectionism whereby painting is understood primarily in terms of interior decoration.

Canaletto, Painter of "vedute"
Giovanni Antonio Canal, called Canaletto, was born in Venice on October 28, 1697 and died in that same city in 1768. His father, Bernardo, was a painter and set designer of a certain renown, and it was under him that young Giovanni Antonio began working as a painter of theater sets. Indeed, they travelled together to Rome in 1719 to execute the sets for Alessandro Scarlatti's *Tito Sempronio Greco* and the *Turno Auricino*. To be a set painter required above all a perfect knowledge of the rules of architectural and illusionistic perspective, as well as an ability to manipulate them pictorially and expressively. Canaletto would no doubt be grateful for this knowledge throughout his career as a veduta painter.
It appears that it was in Rome that Canaletto decided to abandon set paint-

ing and dedicate himself to the art of the veduta, probably inspired by the work of Gaspar van Wittel. From that moment, he began his prodigious output of vedutas, mostly of Venice, alternating them with "capricci," or "imagined views" in which he would combine real and imaginary elements (such as the joining in a single image of ancient monuments nowhere near one another in reality, or the transposition of a church or palace into an open countryside, etc.), with results that were often highly suggestive. In this latter genre of painting, characteristically Venetian, he most likely followed the example of the great Marco Ricci of Belluno (1676–1730). As for veduta painting proper, of which he would later become the most famous practitioner, his model (aside from the aforementioned van Wittel) was the Friulian painter, Luca Carlevarijs, who followed as well in the wake of van Wittel. Carlevarijs had developed a technique of isolating luminous partial views of Venice, establishing the premises for a truly new pictorial genre with his collection of 104 engravings entitled *The Edifices, and Views of Venice Drawn, and Placed in Perspective, and Engraved by Luca Carlevaris* (1703). Like his older colleague, Canaletto laid out his compositions with the help of a camera obscura, a lensed instrument which allowed one to project the image of a given scene onto a surface whereupon, after having passed through a system of mirrors to correct its implicit invertedness, the painter could fix the contour by simply tracing them. The use of a "mechanical" instrument such as this which allowed man in a certain sense to conquer nature, tells us much about the fervent climate of the Venetian Enlightenment, epitomized in the un

Venice from the Motta, pen and dark ink. Windsor, Royal Collections.

abashed enthusiasm of the erudite Francesco Algarotti (1765), who affirms that "... The use made by the Astronomers of the Telescope, and by the Physicists of the Microscope, that same should be made of the Camera Obscura by the painters. All such devices serve to better know and represent Nature." Canaletto's use of the instrument was not, however, quite so scientific, inasmuch as he very often intervened to correct the imprecisions of the image provided by the camera obscura, especially as regards the *arie*, or the light and atmosphere, as his biographer, Zanetti, points out (1771). He also modified and even distorted the perspective toward expressive ends, which would inspire his great contemporary, Michele Marieschi, to develop a species of "wide-angle" perspective for his own Venetian vedutas. This has moved some commentators linked to neoclassical culture (i.e. Ticozzi, 1818) to judge Canaletto harshly for having ventured outside the "limits of the rules of perspective," even while admitting that no one could rival him in "representing objects with more live-liness, or to greater effect." So, "effect" was fine by Ticozzi, but he objects to the transgression of perspectival rigor. This is a very important point for a proper understanding of Canaletto's painting, for up until quite recently his stature was diminished by the stigma of being seen less as a painter than as a "photographer," a mechanical copyist of uninterpreted reality. Only in 1960 did the Italian art historian, C. Brandi, perceive in the painter (the son, we will recall, of a theatrical set painter) anything but "naturalism, manual objectivity, inert virtuosity," despite the use of the camera obscura. Brandi understood that his vistas "have a rather more cerebral, rather less phenomenological origin" than the typical landscapes of his epoch. This critical direction (intuited as we have seen by Ticozzi in 1818, but forgotten thereafter) was taken up by Corboz in 1974 and in the monograph of 1985, aptly titled *Canaletto: Venice Imagined*. Without forcing the reading of an autonomous and coherent genre, we can distinguish at least two tendencies in veduta painting: that of van Wittel and the Roman-

Neapolitan school (whose principal exponents were Hendrik Frans van Lint and Antonio Joli), essentially a faithfully realistic "northern" approach; and that of Canaletto and the Venetians (Bellotto, Marieschi and Guardi), oriented more toward interpretation, and with a strong element of perspective drawing. This interpreted (rather than "imagined") Venice which the latter group presents to us, however, is always an authentic Venice, never completely invented, but rather filtered through the personality of the painter, who may go so far as to distort the architecture, but who will always—at least in the best works—allow the atmosphere to shine fully through.

Canaletto, then, combined his initial experience as a perspective painter and theatrical scenographer, which is immediately evident in his extraordinary drawings (the Gallerie dell'Accademia in Venice conserve a rich album; another large *corpus* is in the English Royal Collection). Drawing is the first moment in Canaletto's approach to the veduta, inasmuch as he would set himself up with his camera obscura, perhaps in Piazza San Marco or on the Rialto Bridge or in some small neighborhood square, and then trace the architectural perspective with a pencil, transferring it to canvas later on in his studio (these drawings, sometimes actually simple sketches, sometimes extremely elaborate, were self-deprecatingly called "doodles" by Canaletto himself). Given the flexibility of this method, it is rather likely that he executed in his Venetian studio the many Roman subjects drawn from life during his sojourn there in 1719–20.

It is also highly probable that the painter based many of his compositions and perspectival framings on the collection of engravings published by Carlevarijs in 1703, which would have constituted a repertoire both formidable and comfortable in that it could be used in the studio. Drawing on these models, Canaletto focused his own research primarily on light, or better, on its intensity and gradations, and this became the signature trait of the better part of his production. Unlike Carlevarijs, who loved to populate his scenes with richly costumed figures, Canaletto gave priority to the architectural aspect, consigning figures to the subordinate function of lending a touch of liveliness, as in the beautiful *Campo San Giacometto* (ca. 1729–30, Dresden Gemäldegalerie; Plate 5), which contains a charming scene of a picture dealer hawking his wares amidst other vignettes of daily life, all beneath a pale sky hung with a wispy veil of clouds. Canaletto's earliest works are distinguished by their strong lighting contrasts and limpid atmosphere, as exemplified in the first four vedutas known to us (once owned by the prince of Liechtenstein, today divided between the Thyssen Collection in Lugano and Ca' Rezzonico in Venice), datable from 1719 to 1723. Among them, the *Canal Grande Looking Northeast, from Palazzo Balbi to the Rialto Bridge* (Plate 1), dominated by the deep grey-green of the water and intense blue of the sky, already demonstrates an exceptional level of quality, while the *Rio dei Mendicanti Looking South* (Plates 2, 3) is by contrast more sober in its tonalities of pinkish greys and blues and its more vaporous atmosphere. Five paintings from this same decade were bought in 1733 by the Prince Elector of Saxony, Augustus II, and are today in the museum of Dresden: apart from the aforementioned *Campo San Giacometto*

Capriccio with Classical Ruins on a Riverbank and Mountains in the Background, pen and black ink over pencil with grey wash. Windsor, Royal Collections.

s a work that stands out for both its quality and compositional originality, the *Church of the Santi Giovanni e Paolo with the School of St. Mark* (Plate 4), characterized by the signature "cross-cut shadow," as Roberto Longhi put it, and its mood of the "useless afternoons" of the Venetian summer.

It was during these years that Canaletto entered into contact with his first important patrons: Stefano Conti of Lucca, for whom he painted between 1725 and 1726 a series of four views of the Canal Grande (now in a private collection in Montreal), and the first of the English *amateurs* who would constitute the core of his future clientele, the bizarre Owen McSwiney, adventurer and man of affairs. The Englishman commissioned Canaletto, together with Giovanni Battista Cimaroli, Giovanni Battista Pittoni and Piazzetta, to execute portions of two scenes from a curious series of twenty-four canvases depicting imaginary monumental tombs of illustrious personages; in each of these (which also involved other important artists of the Veneto like Marco and Sebastiano Ricci, and from Emilia, such as Donato Creti and Francesco Monti), a figure painter, a landscapist and an architectural specialist collaborated, the latter role most likely that entrusted to the young Canaletto. The two canvases to which he contributed (*Capriccio with the Allegorical Tomb of Archbishop Tillotson* and *Capriccio with the Allegorial Tomb of Lord Somers*) are conserved in private collections in Britain. McSwiney, in a series of letters and notes, draws a concise and lively written portrait of the artist, describing his cantankerous and capricious character as that of a *prima donna*, as well as angrily complaining of the outrageous prices he charged for his work. Evidently this did not, however, prevent the painter from insinuating himself into the English market through an extraordinary series of Venetian vedutas, which graced (and in part continue to grace) the residences of the noblest English families.

Still from the fertile years of the 1720s comes the canvas depicting *San Cristoforo, San Michele and Murano Seen from the Fondamenta Nuove* (Plate 9), unprecedented in both its framing of the scene and crepuscular atmosphere, the sky riven by vaporous striations, the last dying ray of sunlight warming the facade of the little church in the distance.

After 1730, Canaletto executed a group of twenty-four vedutas, among which are some of his finest works, that was acquired by the fourth Duke of Bedford and is today conserved in the family residence at Woburn Abbey. By this time, Canaletto had already made the acquaintance of the future English ambassador to Venice, Joseph Smith, a singularly fearless businessman, art dealer, informed and refined collector and animator of the cultural life of Venice, who would soon become the painter's own agent—for at least two years, between 1742 and 1744, Canaletto worked exclusively for him. In his last years, Ambassador Smith sold his exceptional collection of paintings and drawings of the Venetian school to King George III of England. This unmatched bounty, today conserved at Windsor Castle, comprises fifty paintings and one hundred forty-two drawings by Canaletto alone, encompassing practically the entire arc of his career.

Between the end of the 1720s and 1735, he produced a magnificent series of twelve vedutas and two Venetian festivals, commissioned by Joseph Smith and engraved by Visentini (1735). Particularly outstanding are the *Regatta on the Canal Grande* (Plate 15) and the *Return of the Bucintoro on Ascension Day* (Plate 16), this latter being part of the ancient Venetian ceremony of the marriage of the Doge with the sea. Here are some of Canaletto's most chromatically saturated works, with the ships fitted out for the festival and multicolored throngs crowded onto benches and balconies. The first of the two is conceived in terms of depth, the Canal receding radically like a great funnel, while the second uses the opposite scheme of stretching the Canal horizontally along the foreground plane and closing off the distance with the Piazza and the flank of the Palazzo Ducale.

In 1742, the second edition of Visentini's engravings based on the paintings of Canaletto was published (*Prospectu Magni Canalis Venetiarum*). Their number was augmented from fourteen to twenty-four, with the addition of several new vedutas (today in private English collections). This edition carried the dedication "In Aedibus Joseph Smith Angli," and two years later, Canaletto would dedicate to his friend a series of aquatints entitled *Other Views Taken from Other Imagined Places*. It was during this period that Canaletto undertook a number of visits inland (perhaps accompanied by his nephew, the future painter, Bernardo Bellotto) following the Brenta canal toward Padua and feverishly drawing the Veneto countryside. From these drawings were born a series of prints and many beautiful paintings, among which is

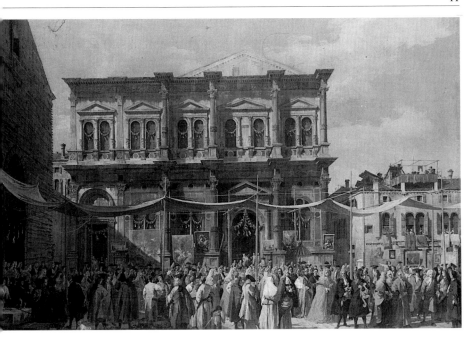

The Doge's Visit to the St. Roch Festival. London, National Gallery. Every year on the saint's day (August 16), an exhibition of paintings took place, an authentic outdoor "group" exhibition of the eighteenth-century Venetian Scuola.

The Locks at Dolo sul Brenta (Plate 10 is one of several known versions), perhaps a point of inspiration and departure for the young and promising Belotto.

The English Sojourn

Canaletto's rapport with England had so intensified, thanks in part to the efforts of the good Consul Smith, that in 1746 the painter embarked for London, where he would stay for fully a decade (if one excludes a brief return home around 1750). The motive that led him to seek out new clientele on their own home turf (probably carrying with him a good number of Venetian "doodles" ready to be translated into paintings) lies in the Austrian War of Succession which had so limited the flow of foreign travelers to Venice, particularly wealthy English ones. Ca-

naletto's London period, long underestimated (at least until Brandi's monograph of 1960), must instead be considered as one of the peaks of his career, the fruit of a rethinking of his early experiences in the context of a profoundly new and different urban, climatic and historical atmosphere. The English vedutas are generally more panoramic in their scope than the Venetian works, with a more open horizon and an even greater attention to detail, perhaps in response to his clients' tastes. One can already recognize the signs of this evolution in works from the late 1730s, such as the majestic masterpiece in the Boston Museum of Fine Arts, *The Basin of San Marco* (Plate 21; from the Collection of the Dukes of Northumberland at Castle Howard), with its overwhelmingly dilated horizontality.

One of the first English vedutas, perhaps from 1746, is *Westminster Bridge Looking South* (Plate 23; New Haven, Yale Center for British Art, Paul Mellon Collection), a disjointed and even clumsy work, conditioned as it is by the long bridge that cuts the composition in two.

Far more interesting are the views of London, which is seen as a boundless city in rapid expansion, teeming with people and activity, totally different from Canaletto's Venice, which was already in the process of surrendering to a supreme state of lethargy.

Canaletto gives us many readings of the city, among which are some exceptional views of the Thames. Particularly noteworthy are *The Thames from the Terrace of Somerset House*, formerly in the Mellon Collection (Plates 24, 25; a preparatory drawing is at Windsor Castle), and the magnificent *The City and St. Paul's Church* (collection of the Duke of Richmond). The painter fully succeeds in characterizing the difference between the urban realities of London and his native Venice, as in *Whitehall and Privy Garden Seen from Richmond House* (Collection of the Duke of Richmond) and *Westminster Abbey with the Procession of the Knights of the Order of Bath* (Plate 26).

One notes in the London paintings a tendency toward monochromy, which in a painter of light and color like Canaletto has always seemed somewhat disconcerting. But what we are in fact seeing here is his precise perception of the absolute irreconcilability of Italian and English realities, which he strives to translate into his canvases. It is clearly not a matter, except perhaps in some sporadic cases, of a decline in his painterly abilities, as has been suggested more than once.

Having returned to Venice not long after 1756 (perhaps following a brief stay in Paris), Canaletto spent his last years in an effort to be accepted into the Accademia.

The painter succeeded only in 1763 five years before his death (the delay was probably owed to the fact that veduta painting was seen as a minor genre and hardly academic), gaining membership by submitting the curious *Capriccio with Colonnade* (Gallerie dell'Accademia; Plate 33).

Canaletto, Painter of "capricci"

After dispelling the myth of the "photographer" painter, absolutely faithful to optical reality, André Corboz (1985) went on to demonstrate the fragility of the apparent dichotomy between the veduta and the capriccio.

Canaletto dedicated himself to both with the same standards of quality and the same poetic energy, evidently never encountering any particularly onerous differences. The capriccio is, after all, simply an imagined veduta, based on real elements which are then recomposed according to the painter's whim.

Thus one finds ancient monuments, in reality quite distant from one another, assembled within the same image, or well-known urban churches and palaces set in real or fantastic landscapes, or further yet, grand architectural projects that were never actually built. This is the case of the *Capriccio with the Rialto Bridge*, which follows an unrealized plan of Palladio's (versions at Windsor Castle and the Galleria Nazionale in Parma; Plate 22) and which demonstrates close connections with the ideas of Francesco Algarotti and Joseph Smith, both of whom were great admirers of Palladio. Evidently,

he discussions between Smith and Ca-
aletto were not exclusively commer-
ial in nature, but intellectual as well.
he version in Parma includes other
alladian buildings such as Palazzo
Chiericati and the Logge di Vicenza,
hus rendering it an homage to the
reat 16th-century architect and at the
ame time suggesting an incipient neo-
lassicism.

rom his earliest years as a painter, Ca-
aletto had been producing classiciz-
1g capricci, such as those featuring
Loman monuments taken from his
journey there in 1719, to which he
rould often refer over the course of
is career.

he taste for depicting ancient ruins in
naginary settings was introduced in
Venice by Marco Ricci and enjoyed
reat commercial success; Canaletto's
rilliant contemporary, the painter Mi-
hele Marieschi (1710–1743), also alter-
ated between the production of ca-
ricci and vedutas.

he kinds of capricci Canaletto loved
est were those based on real elements
rawn from life and then "decontex-
1alized," broken up and recomposed
ke puzzles, repeated many times in
ifferent versions, as in the *Capriccio
ith Classical Ruins and Renaissance
uildings* (Rome, Banca Nazionale del
Lavoro; Plate 29), or the numerous
ariations on the *Capriccio with Classical
Motifs* in the Museo Poldi Pezzoli in Mi-
ln (Plates 30, 31).

)ccupying the space between the par-
llel lines defining the veduta and
ne capriccio are works like *The Arch
f Constantine with the Colosseum* (Mali-
u, J. Paul Getty Museum; Plate 28),
ne in a series of five paintings of Ro-
nan subjects. Occasionally, Classical
uildings and ruins are set in the Ve-
etian lagoon, as in the *Capriccio with*

Lagoon in St. Louis Art Museum (Plate
34).

The Legacy

After having been lauded by his con-
temporaries, among whom he had become widely renowned, Canaletto fell
out of critical favor and remained
there for more than a century. Even
just a few years after his death, the
great 18th-century art historian, Luigi
Lanzi, would dedicate only a brief pas-
sage of his *Pictorial History of Italy* to Canaletto, observing with his usual dis-
cretion and aplomb that in Canaletto's
paintings "the average spectator sees
nature, while the connoisseur sees art.
This he possessed in eminent measure." The compliment notwithstanding, Lanzi still considered veduta
painting as a minor genre.

The lowest point in the course of Canaletto's critical fortune came in the 19th
century with his famous defamation at
the hands of the English critic, John
Ruskin, who, drunk with Romantic
sentiment, was hardly in a position to
appreciate the Enlightenment-era art
of Canaletto. There followed several
decades of genuine oblivion, until the
earliest attempts at rediscovery in the
opening years of this century. It was fi-
nally Roberto Longhi (1946) who, in a
few lucid lines, reopened history's eyes
to the true greatness of Canaletto, even
when compared with the most honor-
ed European masters. From that moment on, there has been a continuous
flowering of essays, monographs and
exhibitions—from the volumes by
Brandi (1960), Constable (1962), and
Corboz (1985) to the retrospectives in
Venice (1967; 1982) and New York
(1989)—all of which confirm his rank
among the greatest exponents of 18th-
century Italian painting.

Where to See Canaletto

Over the course of a half-century of activity, Antonio Canaletto produced many hundreds of paintings, drawings and engravings—an extraordinarily copious output made even more so by the efficiency of his working method and by his practice of replicating compositions, often crossing over from one medium to another. An additional factor which contributed to such prodigiousness is that his paintings (all of them oil on canvas), despite their exceptional precision and scope, are for the most part rather small. Only in rare cases do they reach dimensions in excess of two meters in width.

Today we can count approximately three hundred fifty canvases attributable with reasonable certainty to the master. Two thirds of this total are in private collections, most of them English. This is explained by the fact that Canaletto's production was aimed specifically at private collectors who tended to buy finished paintings rather than commission them (the cases of Joseph Smith and the Duke of Bedford, who commissioned works directly for their own collections, are the exception rather than the rule). One can reasonably say that a good half of Canaletto's known works are in Great Britain, thanks to the decade spent working in London and to the incessant collecting of English clients. Conversely, the works remaining in Italy barely make up a sixth of Canaletto's oeuvre.

The master never veered from his chosen path as a painter of vedute and ca-pricci (though the majorit of capricci belong to his ear lier years). As for the ved utas drawn from realit (keeping in mind the cau tion with which the notio of "realism" must be applie to Canaletto's urban imag es), his guiding muse wa above all the city of Venic itself, with its countless hid den corners and breathtak ing vistas, all of then heightened by the magica light of sea and sky. Th most significant groups o non-Venetian works are th canvases depicting famou Roman monuments and th views of London and th English countryside Though rare, and for thi reason particularly valua ble, Canaletto also execute a number of landscapes o the Veneto inland, especial ly of the towns along th Brenta canal.

Works in Italy

The canvases by Canalett still in Italy number aroun sixty, with more than half i private collections. For thi reason, it is rather difficu to provide a manageabl itinerary. We will limit our selves, then, to the most im portant of the few painting on public display.

Lombardy

The paintings by Canalett in the hands of Milanes private collectors are of ex ceptional importance, suc that the Lombardian capita must be considered funda mental for an understand ing of the master, even i many are not accessible t the public. Outstandin among these are the tw largest and most elaborat canvases painted by Cana letto, *The Arrival of the Impe al Ambassador* and the *Re-rn of the Bucintoro*, con-rved in the Collezione respi.

he Pinacoteca di Brera osts two rather small ved-tas of excellent quality: *The asin of San Marco* and *The anal Grande Seen from Cam-* ● *San Vio*. A *Capriccio with uins* and a view of the *Prato lla Valle in Padua* are con-rved in the Museo Poldi ezzoli. The Galleria del-Accademia Carrara in Ber-amo, which houses the leg-y of important private col-ctions, owns a pair of views f the Canal Grande.

enice
he canvases by Canaletto the museums of his native ty are a mere three: two arly vedutas of the Canal rande, in the Museo del ettecento Veneziano in Ca' ezzonico, and the late *Ca-riccio with Colonnade*, sub-itted to the Accademia as application for a profes-rship in perspective, to-ay conserved in the Galle-e dell'Accademia.
the paucity of works re-aining in Venice seems aradoxical, the truth of the atter is that Canaletto orked almost exclusively or foreign tourists and col-ctors (especially English), nd had almost no market his homeland.

ome
oman museums conserve veral traces of Canaletto's arly activity. A singular *erspective View* is in the Ac-ademia di San Luca. In the alleria Borghese are the *olosseum* and the *Forum*, at-ibuted by some to Bernar-o Bellotto. A lovely group f four Venetian vedutas is nserved in the Galleria

Nazionale in the Palazzo Barberini.

Other locations in Italy
The Galleria degli Uffizi in Florence hosts two notewor-thy capricci, the early *View of the Canal Grande from Palazzo Balbi*, and a version of *The Basin of San Marco*.
In the Galleria Sabauda in Turin hangs an interesting early canvas, *Docks with the Palazzo Ducale*.
Lastly, the Pinacoteca Na-zionale in Parma conserves one of Canaletto's true gems, the *Capriccio with Pal-ladian Buildings*, in which several of the architect's most famous works are set in the context of the Canal Grande.

Works Located Abroad
As mentioned before, the great majority of Canalet-to's works on canvas is dis-persed among private col-lections and foreign mu-seums. The list is endless, an indication of the Venetian's success throughout the world. The predominant role, thought, is assumed by Great Britain, where nearly two hundred fifty canvases by the master are conserved in public, royal, aristocratic and private collections.

Great Britain
The richest single group of works is undoubtedly that of the Royal Collections, which count some sixty paintings by Canaletto. The major part are conserved at Windsor Castle where, apart from two vedutas of *London Seen from the Thames* and a series of *Roman Monu-ments*, the collection consists prevalently of *Views of Ven-ice*, many of which originally belonged to Joseph Smith.

Especially noteworthy are a group of vedutas datable to around 1730, and the singu-lar *Interior of the Basilica of San Marco*.
Of extraordinary historical importance is the sequence of twenty-four splendid *Views of Venice* commis-sioned by the Duke of Bed-ford during his visit to Ven-ice in 1731, conserved today in the family collection at Woburn Abbey. Many of these were used as models for engravings, such as the *Towers of the Arsenale* and *Campo Santa Maria Formosa*. London's Wallace Collec-tion hosts a rich series of eleven canvases, among which is the monumental *Piazza San Marco Looking to-ward San Geminiano*. The National Gallery counts a dozen works, several of them masterpieces; the *Stoneyard at San Vidal* marks a turning point in Canalet-to's career, as does the daz-zling *Visit of the Doge to San Rocco*; from the London pe-riod are the *Rotonda of Rane-lagh* and the *King's College Chapel at Eton*, one of the finest portrayals of the En-glish countryside.
The famous *Procession of the Knights of the Order of Bath* is conserved at Westminster Abbey, itself accurately de-picted in the painting. The paintings gallery at Dulwich College hosts the interesting image of the *Old Walton Bridge*.
Two views of Piazza San Marco and the courtyard of the Palazzo Ducale, distin-guished by the unusual point of view beneath a dar-kened loggia, are conserved in the Fitzwilliam Museum in Cambridge. Not to be outdone is rival Oxford, whose Ashmolean Museum

boasts the enchanting canvas of the *Locks at Dolo*. The National Galleries of Wales and Ireland both possess vedutas by Canaletto.

Among the private collections, the most worthy of note are those of the dukes of Northumberland, Buccleuch, Richmond and Norfolk, as well as the Neave collection, Atramont.

United States and Canada

As an appendix to the phenomenon of Anglo-Saxon collecting, important works by Canaletto can be found in many North American museums.

The Boston Museum of Fine Arts boasts an unsurpassable masterpiece, *The Basin of San Marco*, an enormous work of unusually broad panoramic scope. The two canonical vedutas of *Piazza San Marco* and the *Entrance of the Canal Grande* are in Washington's National Gallery.

The Ringling Museum in Sarasota possesses two late vedutas, distinguished by a spectacular virtuosity of compositional framing, while the Wadsworth Athenaeum in Hartford has one of the very earliest works of the master, a *Landscape with Ruins*. Also noteworthy are the paintings conserved in Palm Beach, Toledo, Houston, Philadelphia, El Paso, Detroit, Kansas City and Minneapolis.

The National Gallery of Canada in Ottawa hosts a late version of the *Campo San Giacometto* and an unusual *View of Piazza San Marco with the Clock Tower*. The Museum of Montreal features a spectacular *Interior of the Basilica of San Marco*.

Germany, Austria and Switzerland

Humble in quantity but superb in quality are the paintings by Canaletto in German museums. In Berlin are two *Views with the Church of Santa Maria della Salute*, while Dresden's Gemäldegalerie hosts five canvases by the master, the most famous of which is the moving *Campo San Giacometto*, actually an unremarkable subject painted with remarkable suggestiveness. One of the very first views of *Piazza San Marco* is in the Alte Pinakothek in Munich; Leipzig hosts two capricci; another capriccio with Paduan architectural motifs is found in Hamburg's Kunsthalle.

The Kunsthistorisches Museum in Vienna conserves a matched pair of vedutas (the *Punta della Dogana* and *Riva degli Schiavoni*), characterized by a great compositional freedom and unusual framing. The Buehrle collection in Zurich owns three Venetian vedutas originally in the prestigious Buccleuch collection.

Other Locations

From Sao Paolo to Melbourne, from Havana to Stockholm, from Mexico City to Moscow—of the numerous paintings by Canaletto which have made their way into every corner of the world, the following are most worthy of note: a pair of *Views of the Thames* in the Narodny Galerie, Prague; two late and evocative *Views of the Lagoon*, and the festive *Reception of the French Ambassador* in the Hermitage, St. Petersburg; a large-scale *Entrance to the Canal Grande* in Grenoble.

1. Canal Grande Looking
Northeast, from Palazzo
Balbi to the Rialto Bridge,
*ca. 1719–23, oil on canvas,
144 × 207 cm. Venice,
Ca' Rezzonico.*

2

2, 3. Rio dei Mendicanti
Looking South, *ca. 1719–
23, oil on canvas, 143 × 200
cm. Venice, Ca' Rezzonico.
This and the preceding
colorplate, along with the two
works in the Thyssen
Collection* (Piazza San
Marco *and* Canal Grande
Looking East from Campo
San Vio) *constitute the
earliest group of vedutas by
Canaletto, once part of the
Royal Collection of
Liechtenstein. The two scenes
operate within different
chromatic schemes, suggesting
a certain experimentalism—
blue-green in the first, and
silver-grey in the second. One
notes a debt to the lighting and
compositional framing of
Carlevarijs, as well as to the
strong tonal contrasts
of Marco Ricci.*

4

4. Church of Santi
Giovanni e Paolo with
the School of St. Mark,
*ca. 1729–30, oil on canvas,
125 × 165 cm. Dresden,
Gemäldegalerie.
This important early work is
the first of a series dedicated to
the Venice's famed* campo,
*or square, as defined by the
facade of a great church. The
clarity and pallor of the colors
and the more liquid brushwork
distinguish this canvas from
those of Canaletto's first
period, which had been
dominated by dark colors and
intense* chiaroscuro *contrasts.
The painting was acquired
along with four other vedutas
(including Plate 5) by
Augustus III of Saxony
in 1733.*

. Campo San Giacometto
(San Giacomo di Rialto),
c. 1729–30, oil on canvas,
95.5 × 117 cm. Dresden,
Gemäldegalerie.
The canvas depicts Venice's
oldest church, whose
foundations were laid in the
12th century. Of particular
interest is the scene in the
center of the picture seller
surrounded by a small crowd,
flanked on the far right by the
stands of travelling vendors.
Along with colorplate 4, this
is one of the masterpieces of
Canaletto's second period,
distinguished by an ever more
transparent light and a
softening of the shadows.

6

6. Stoneyard at San Vidal,
*ca. 1727, oil on canvas,
124 × 163 cm. London,
National Gallery.
The relationship between the
stonecutters at work and the
architectural ambient signals
Canaletto's conquest of a new
sense of space and light. The
campanile in the distance,
which collapsed in 1741,
is part of the church of the
Carità. Across from it
is the Accademia Bridge.*

8. Return of the Bucintoro
on Ascension Day,
*1726–27, oil on canvas,
187 × 259 cm. Moscow,
Pushkin Museum.*
*This painting once belonged to
Catherine II of Russia,
together with its "pendant,"*
the Reception of the French
Ambassador at the Palazzo
Ducale *(St. Petersburg,
Hermitage). The subject was
often reproduced by Canaletto;
the most famous version is in
the Crespi collection in Milan.
The painting describes the
ancient ceremony of the
"Marriage with the Sea," held
every year on Ascension Day,
whereupon the Doge would
toss a gold ring into the lagoon
from his flagship, the
Bucintoro.*

. Piazza San Marco, *1720–
2, oil on canvas, 73.6 × 94
m. New York, Private
Collection.*
*n its recent appearance on the
market bearing an attribution
o Michele Marieschi
Christie's, New York, May
1, 1991), this canvas was
ightly reattributed to the
oung Canaletto by Dario
ucci* (Il Giornale dell'Arte,
1, *July-August 1991, p.49).
The scholar was able to
onvincingly date the painting
n the basis of two objective
acts, rare in the problematic
hronology of Canaletto's*

*work: in the distant
background, the campanile
of San Giorgio Maggiore is
depicted as it was prior to
the remodelling of 1726–28;
furthermore, Piazza San
Marco is still paved with the
bricks that were substituted
with the present pavement
in 1724. In addition,
examination of the painting
technique confirms Succi's
attribution in that the
brushwork is very close
to the Ca' Rezzonico/Thyssen
quartet, until now considered
the earliest known work
by the master.*

9

9. San Cristoforo, San Michele and Murano Seen from the Fondamenta Nuove, *ca. 1725–30, oil on canvas, 142 × 150 cm. Dallas, Museum of Art. The subject of this recently discovered work is rather uncommon, even within the broad panorama of Canaletto's subject matter. The distinctive play of light, the pale striations of vaporous clouds in the dusky sky, the atmosphere of silence and order—all suggest that the work dates from an early, but not quite intitial period, when Canaletto's chromatic contrasts were more intense than we find here. This work should therefore be contemporary with, or just after the Dresden group. Another version, with slight variations, is conserved in the Hermitage in St. Petersburg.*

10

10. The Locks at Dolo sul Brenta, *ca. 1728–29, oil on canvas, 61 × 95 cm. Oxford, Ashmolean Museum.*
The powerful contrasts and brilliant color of this magnificent veduta would seem to resolve its controversial date by linking it stylistically to Canaletto's inland journey toward the end of the 1720s. Other versions of this same subject do exist; the most important, conserved in the Staatsgalerie in Stuttgart, is the chronologically closest one to the Oxford version. Canaletto made another inland voyage in the early 1740s, accompanied by his young nephew, Bernardo Bellotto, from which he drew inspiration for some twenty engravings and numerous paintings.

11

11, 12. Campo Santa Maria
Formosa, *ca. 1730–35, oil
on canvas, 41 × 80 cm.
Woburn Abbey, The Marquess
of Tavistock and Trustees
of the Bedford Estates.*

13

13, 14. The School of St. Roch, *ca. 1730–35, oil on canvas, 41 × 80 cm. Woburn Abbey, The Marquess of Tavistock and Trustees of the Bedford Estates.*
This and the preceding image constitute two of the twenty-four vedutas featuring famous buildings and piazze *acquired, beginning in 1732, by the fourth Duke of Bedford for his residence at Woburn Abbey, paid for through Joseph Smith between 1733 and 1736* *(the English ambassador to Venice acted for several years as Canaletto's agent in the British market). Several of these works, including this one, were engraved by Visentini in 1742. Two drawings which seem to be studies of the view of Santa Maria Formosa are conserved at Windsor Castle, along with some lively related sketches at the Gallerie dell'Accademia in Venice.*

15

15. Regatta on the Canal
Grande, *ca. 1730–35, oil
on canvas, 77 × 126 cm.
Windsor, Royal Collections.*

6

6. Return of the
Bucintoro on Ascension
Day, *ca. 1730–35, oil on
canvas, 77 × 125 cm.
Windsor, Royal Collections.
These two representations
f traditional Venetian
ceremonies belong to a series
of fourteen vedutas of the
Canal Grande painted by
Canaletto and engraved by
Antonio Visentini*
Prospectus Magni Canalis
Venetiarum, *published in
1735), which reached the
Royal Collections through
Joseph Smith's sale
of his private collection to the
King. The art historian, W.J.
Constable (1962),
convincingly suggests that the
Regatta was inspired by a
work of Luca Carlevarijs, the
Regatta in Honor of
Frederick IV of Denmark
in 1709.*

17

17. Canal Grande with the Rialto Bridge, *ca. 1733–35, oil on canvas, 68.5 × 92 cm. Rome, Galleria Nazionale. This work is part of a series of four vedutas (the others:* Piazza San Marco, Canal Grande from the Rialto Bridge Looking toward Ca' Foscari, The Piazzetta Looking South*), all conserved in Rome's Galleria Nazionale and generally datable to the moment immediately following the Woburn Abbey group. Canaletto would repeat this subject in 1744 (the location of which has been unknown since it left the Trotti collection in Paris).*

18

18. Canal Grande Seen
from Campo San Vio, *ca.*
1740, oil on canvas, 53 × 70
cm. Milan, Pinacoteca
di Brera.

9

9. The Pier at San Marco,
a. 1740, oil on canvas,
3.5 × 71 cm. Milan,
Pinacoteca di Brera.
Both this and the preceding
painting are autograph
replicas of canvases conserved
in a private collection in Sao
Paolo, Brazil, which are
themselves based, with
modifications, on two even
earlier works (dated by

Constable to the early 1730s).
Canaletto tended to make
numerous copies of his more
famous subjects, usually in
order to satisfy the exigencies
of his English clients, though
always maintaining the highest
quality. Windsor Castle
conserves a drawing which is
probably a study for this
particular work.

20

20. Fonteghetto della Farina, *ca. 1735–40, oil on canvas, 66 × 112 cm. Venice, Giustiniani Collection.*
This subject, quite rare in Canaletto's oeuvre, is known only in one other smaller painted version (Boston, Museum of Fine Arts) and in a few drawings conserved at Windsor Castle, the compositional framings of which are, however, different from the Giustiniani canvas. *The dating of the work is attested by the soft, blonde light and the pale, attenuated shadows which we associate with the artist's full maturity.*

21

22

22. Capriccio with the
Rialto Bridge, *ca. 1743–44,*
oil on canvas, 56 × 79 cm.
Parma, Galleria Nazionale.
This "imagined veduta"
depicts the famous bridge as it
would have appeared had the
reconstruction project of the
16th century, designed by
Andrea Palladio, ever been
realized. Unlike the analogous
version in the Royal
Collections at Windsor Castle,
this canvas incorporates other
works by Palladio — Palazzo
Chiericati and Vicenza
Basilica.

21. The Basin of San
Marco, *1738–40, oil on*
canvas, 124.5 × 204.5 cm.
Boston, Museum of Fine Arts.
One of Canaletto's most
famous works, it is considered
a masterpiece both for its depth
of observation and
monumental dimensions. Here
Canaletto begins to "dilate"
the space as if viewing the
scene through a wide-angle

lens, expanding its panoramic
scope and lowering the horizon
line, as he would later do
during his English period.
More than half of the canvas
is occupied by the sky, which
serves to emphasize the
spectacular sense of solemnity
emanated by the work, but
which stands in sharp contrast
to the lower part, teeming with
meticulously described activity.

23

23. Westminster Bridge Looking South, *1746, oil on canvas, 96 × 127.5 cm. New Haven, Yale Center for British Art, Paul Mellon Collection. This work is generally thought to be among the very first English vedutas, perhaps datable to 1746, the year Canaletto arrived there (indeed, there exists an engraved copy of this painting by R. Parr dated 1747). The scene describes the naval parade of Lord Mayor of London, a ceremony which took place every year on October 29. The abruptness of the compositional split created by the bridge and the graphic, rather than painterly handling perhaps indicate the painter's unease in the face of a completely new landscape.*

24

24, 25. The Thames from the Terrace of Somerset House, *ca. 1747–55, oil on canvas, 40.5 × 70.5 cm. Private Collection.*
This veduta, which recently appeared on the London art market *(Christie's, November 17, 1989) differs from the majority of Venetian works in that Canaletto privileges the panoramic view of the seemingly endless city, lowering the horizon and* giving over more than half of the painted surface to the sky. Other versions are conserved in the Windsor Royal Collections, and at Cirencester Stowell Park, Collection of Lady Vestey.

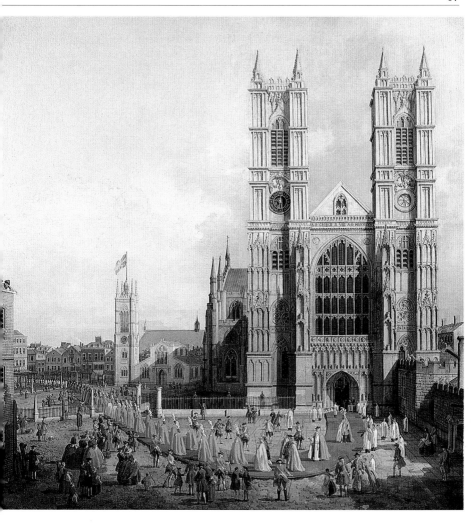

5. Westminster Abbey
ith the Procession of the
nights of the Order of
ath, *1747–55, oil on
nvas, 99 × 101 cm.
ndon, Westminster Abbey.*

27

27. View of Warwick
Castle, *1747–55, oil on
canvas, 72.5 × 136 cm.
Warwick, Warwick Collection.*

28

29

28. The Arch of
Constantine with the
Colosseum, *1742–45, oil
on canvas, 82 × 122 cm.
Malibu, J. Paul Getty
Museum.*
*This image occupies a midway
point between the veduta and
the capriccio, in that it
combines real elements with
imaginary ones. It is possible
that Canaletto based the
painting on drawings executed
during his Roman sojourn
of 1719–20, since it does not
seem that he ever returned
there (or he might have
availed himself of drawings by
his nephew, Bernardo Bellotto,
documented in Rome
in 1742).*

29. Capriccio with Classical
Ruins and Renaissance
Buildings, *ca. 1751–56,
oil on canvas, 81 × 115 cm.
Rome, Banca Nazionale
del Lavoro.*
*Datable perhaps to the second
English period, this work
combines elements of Roman
architecture (the hybrid of the
Pantheon and Palladio's Villa
Rotonda, the ruins of the
Temple of Saturn in the
Forum) with Gothic and
Renaissance structures (the
campanile to the right was
identified by Corboz as that
of the English Gothic church
of St. Dunstan-in-the-East).*

30

30, 31. Capriccio with
Classical Motifs, *ca. 1740–
50, oil on canvas, 91 × 125
cm. Milan, Museo Poldi
Pezzoli.*
*This is one of the most often-
repeated compositions in all
of Canaletto's oeuvre, with
approximately twenty known
versions, some autograph and*
*others workshop productions.
This work, of uncertain date,
is surely a re-elaboration of the
Classical motifs recorded by
Canaletto during his stay in
Rome (1719–20). The arch
in the background is clearly
inspired by the Arch
of Constantine.*

32

32. Capriccio with Paduan Motifs, *ca. 1735–40, oil on canvas, 63 × 76.5 cm. Florence, Palazzo Vecchio. This work, along with the* Capriccio with Roman Motifs, *once belonged to the Contini Bonacossi Collection in Florence. Seized by the Nazis and recovered in 1948 by Rodolfo Siviero, the paintings depict real buildings from Padua and Rome, together with invented ones, in totally imaginary settings, in keeping with one of Canaletto's most commercially successful formulae. Approximately fifteen replicas of these paintings are known to exist, many of them difficult to date and some of uncertain authenticity.*

33. Capriccio with Colonnade, *signed and dated 1765, oil on canvas, 131 × 93 cm. Venice, Gallerie dell'Accademia. This work describes the atrium and grand staircase of a Venetian palazzo, and betrays Canaletto's wish to present himself above all as a perspective painter. That notwithstanding, as Edwards observes in his* List of the Painters of the Accademia *(1812), the "intelligence of the play of light and shadow, with all the virtuosity of the master artist" make this, rather than a mere demonstration of craftsmanship, a painting of enormous quality and fascination.*

34

34. Capriccio with Lagoon, *ca. 1745–50, oil on canvas, 51 × 68 cm. St. Louis Art Museum.*

A serene and expansive imaginary landscape, suffused with the dying light of the sun, the pale white moon rising off to the left. The campanile seems inspired by that of San Rocco in the town of Dolo, while the pavilion on the right is reminiscent of similar structures in Padua (the Porta Portello, for example). Attributed by some art historians to Bernardo Bellotto, the date of this capriccio, as with all works of its type, has long been debated. But the research generated by the great 1989 retrospective in New York convincingly presents the work as a rather late Canaletto, painted sometime after his inland journey of the early 1740s.

Anthology of Comments

He masters all that has ever existed [...] His manner is luminous, gay, lively, transparent and admirably meticulous. The English have pampered this artist to such a degree, offering him three times more than what he himself asks for his paintings, that it is no longer possible to buy anything from him.
(Charles de Brosses, *Lettres familières... de l'Italie*, 1739)

The multitude of works he has executed for English nobles and gentlemen has brought him great fame, and he is highly esteemed for his great skill in this genre.
(G. Vertue, *Notebooks*, 1746)

The rays of light which proceed from objects, after entering the pupil, pass through the crystalline humor, whose form and size are like that of a lentil. Here they are refracted and then united in the retina which is found on the back of the eye; and here they reproduce the image of the object toward which the pupil is directed; whereupon the soul, in some way or other, grasps this image and perceives it [...] By way of a lens of glass and a mirror is made a device which transports any image or painting [...] onto a fine sheet of paper, where others can see it in all its perfection, and contemplate it [...] Without the assistance of any light other than that of the object one wishes to capture, the image achieves a clarity and a power beyond words [...] And let us then praise the correctness of the contours, the verity of the perspective and lights and shadows, which one

could neither improve nor even conceive; the color is of a liveliness and warmth that is unsurpassable. The principal features of the figures are strong and bright in the parts most exposed to the light, diminishing gradually and imperceptibly into shadow. The shadows are deep, but not crude, just as the contours are not too sharp, but precise [...] When we look at a single object to consider it, it is surrounded by many others, which at the same time reach our eye, which do not allow us to clearly distinguish all the modulations of color and light of the single object [...] Where by contrast with the Camera Obscura the visual force is concentrated entirely on that single object, eliminating every other source of light [...]
Nothing else demonstrates this better than the Camera Obscura, in which Nature paints the objects closest to the eye with brushstrokes of such acuity and fixity, and those far away with gradually softer strokes [...]
The use made by the Astronomers of the Telescope, by the Physicists of the Microscope, that same use should be made of the Camera Obscura by the painters. All such devices serve equally to better know and represent Nature.
(F. Algarotti, *Raccolta di Lettere sopra la Pittura e l'Architettura*, 1765)

Canal[etto] taught by his example the true use of the camera obscura; and to recognize the defects which result in a painting when the painter trusts entirely the perspective given to him by the device, and the colors, especially of the atmosphere, not understanding how much they offend the senses [...] Canal united in his paintings nature and pictorial license with great economy, which in his true works are evident to he who has the good sense to judge them; and he who understands painting finds in them great art in the choice of sites, in the distribution of the figures, in the city squares, in the handling of shadows and light; in addition to a clarity and lively skill with color and brush, reflections of a serene mind and felicitous genius.

(A.M. Zanetti, *Della pittura veneziana e delle opere pubbliche de' veneziani maestri*, 1771)

Born to Bernardo, painter of theater sets, he followed his father's profession and acquired through its practice an eccentricity of thought and an immediacy of painting, which he then applied to innumerable minor works. Bored by his father's trade, he went as a youth to Rome, where he dedicated himself to painting views from nature and especially ancient ruins.

Once returned to Venice, he continued this same study of views of that city, which nature and art conspired to render the most magnificent and innovative in the world. He painted a great many of them, as he saw them; pleasing to the curiosity of those who could not see the Queen of the Adriatic with their own eyes. He also painted many works of his own invention; a gracious mixture of the modern and the ancient, of the real and the capricious.

Some of these he made for Algarotti. The most instructive and innovative of all seems to me that of the Canal Grande with the great Rialto Bridge designed by Palladio taking the place of the existing one; and is surrounded by the Vicenza Basilica and Palazzo Chericato, works by Palladio, and other buildings chosen and disposed according to the taste of that great and cultured man who has contributed so much to the improvement of art and taste both within and outside Italy. In executing his perspectives Canaletto availed himself of the camera obscura for its exactitude, yet he amended its defects, especially in the tones of the atmosphere.

He was the first to teach its true use, limiting it to only that which is most pleasing. He was fond of grand effects, and in producing them took the example of Tiepolo, who sometimes painted figures for him; and everything he touched with his brush, whether buildings, water, clouds or figures, he invested with a vigor that seems to bring out their most impressive aspects.

He exercized a certain painterly freedom, though only such that the average viewer sees nature there, and the connoisseur sees art. This latter he possessed in eminent measure.

(L. Lanzi, *Storia pittorica della Italia*, 1796)

The mannerism of Canaletto is the most deplorable I know in all the world of art. Exercizing the most servile and fatuous imitation, he imitates nothing but the vacuity of shadows, nor does he give form to individual architectural features, however exact they may seem [...] Neither myself nor anyone else would have dared to speak a word against him: but in truth he is a small, bad painter [...] Canaletto does not possess any quality except that of being able to imitate the most ordinary effects of light and shadow.

(J. Ruskin, *Modern Painters*, 1843–60, ed. 1897)

The great Antonio Canal (unfortunately represented in this exhibition solely by the perspective study he was obliged to paint in order to be accepted by the Venetian academicians) began by painting dry Roman *vedute* in the tradition of Vanvitelli and Panini; later, in the interest of verisimilitude, he availed himself of the "camera obscura," and it was then, miraculously, that he began to approach true poetry.

When one recalls that, sixty years earlier in Venice, the best landscape painting being done was that of Monsù Cussin, while in Holland Vermeer was painting his *View of Delft*, one realizes that Canaletto was responsible for restoring the stature of Venetian painting to a European level. His Enlightenment-era certainty of absolute truth, expressed through the gilded light and cross-cut shadows of useless afternoons in a Venice that crumbles and cracks like the deepest incisions of his admirable aquatints, has the stereoscopic wistfulness of the painted vistas of the "New World."

(R. Longhi, *Viatico per cinque*

ecoli di pittura veneziana, .946, ed. 1978)

In the past, when considering Canaletto's use of he camera obscura, it was hown to be an expedient vhich served him as an *effraction* of nature, rather han as a *transcription*. Yet oday his historical *curriculum* is still posed in the same dentical terms. It is symptomatic that 18th-century veduta painting in general—not just Canaletto—focuses on *quadraturismo*, on he exploitation of perspective toward illusionistic :nds. These vedutas, for vhich one is compelled or 1ot compelled to find a *renre* in the literary sense, 1ave a rather more intellectual than phenomenological origin than other, similar andscapes. What we have 1ere is clearly a perspectival .keleton which is gradually 1nvested with visual appearance. The fact that this skel-:ton then remains a skele-on—very few other pain-ers were able to represent he originary interiority of a vision in the process of be-:oming an image—does not ilter the simultaneous birth of two types of images, first of which arrives at illu-sionism, the other at pure reality. But in this sense there can 3e no doubt that, in the :arly Canaletto, one must ook more toward the hid-den influence of the scenog-rapher Bibbiena, rather than the narrowly optical vi-sion of Vanvitelli. One needs only recall the composition of one of Canaletto's earliest veduta paintings, the *San Cristoforo della Pace and San Michele* in the English Royal Collections, in order to rec-ognize the scenographic ex-pedient of the framing of the stair, extraordinarily re-established in the irrefut-able evidence of that light and those shadows [...] This radically *new* way of see-ing—new only because it is a renewed way of bringing oneself back to the roots of artistic creation—Canaletto owes neither to Vanvitelli nor to the torpid Carleva-rijs, even if he shamelessly steals from the latter fram-ings, dispositions, passages: in other words, scenogra-phy, yet one more time sce-nography is adapted from the Friulian painter/mathe-matician and transformed into pleasant Venetian ved-utas. This mode of "realiza-tion," in the sense of making things true—if we can allow for just a moment the meta-phorical use of that inap-propriate term—has no precedent in Venetian or Italian or French painting, neither in Canaletto's time nor previously.
(C. Brandi, *Canaletto*, 1960)

The complex personality of Antonio Canal, whose true aspirations are not merely suggested, but truly manifested in his drawings, expresses itself in painterly practice by de-grees. In the large-scale paintings from the Crespi Collection, magnificent for their chromatic vivacity and for the directness and preci-sion of their contact with the world of reality, Canaletto takes up iconographical themes already addressed by Luca Carlevarijs and, like his predecessor, imposes a narrative character upon them: but what new force, what open and boundless sense of nature and of ob-jects he is able to reveal! Fi-nally he gives birth to the pure veduta, to a sincere and unadulterated reality, scrutinized in its truest and most profound essence, and from that moment on, his views of the city by the sea bud until the blossoming of that incomparable poetic vi-sion, the *Basin of San Marco* in Boston.
(*I vedutisti veneziani del Sette-cento*, catalogue of the exhi-bition, edited by P. Zampet-ti, 1967)

The partisans of the coin-cidence of image and reality live in a mythical world, in which the mere presentation of an object guarantees its reality. Those among them who repeat as an article of faith the refrain of Canaletto's literalism, willing victims of the *effect of reality*, systematically con-found *precision* (of painting) with *exactitude* (of "observa-tion"). Certain that the real resembles Canaletto as much as he is faithful to the real, it would seem that they have not noticed the vision Canaletto introduced to Venice between 1730 and 1740, the probable motive for Levey's characterization of "his maniacal, almost spinsterish precision." What they fail to recognize is that the operation of painting produces a more coherent image than the spectacle from which it is drawn [...] Certainly the "superimpos-ability" of image and specta-cle was a source of amaze-ment at the time: "Master Ant. Canale, who, in this country, astonishes abso-lutely everyone who sees his works," writes Marchesini, insisting on Canaletto's real-ism in 1725, well before his "photographic manner" had arrived at its final formula. And when the formula was applied, it was hailed as the revelation of a universal truth heretofore concealed and finally communicated, thanks to the skill of Canaletto, efficacious and "inimitable" (therefore imitated). For this reason it is difficult to agree with Gioseffi when he states not only that Canal introduced the "paradigm of photographic truth" to painting, but that his innovation drove others to take this into account. That point of view, in fact, did not take hold: only a few minor veduta painters attempted mediocre imitations. Bellotto, as much as he may have experimented with his uncle's technique, turned the language of Canaletto toward other ends as soon as he established himself in Germany; Guardi satisfied himself with a studied *sfumato* and disarticulation. [...] It remains to be demonstrated through the works themselves that Canaletto is not a species of freehand photographer, and that his vedutas, as recognized in his own time, are rather *belle infideli* ("gorgeous untruths") [...] Between capriccio and veduta there is no difference but one of degree. One sees this so clearly at the compositional level that the antinomy cannot be sustained, not even at the conceptual level. Canal preferred to stay within the bounds of the genres, so that the variation would not disturb the perception of the real, or would not be perceptible without a control, functioning like an instrument that discloses the evidence of the painting rather than that of the city. In all his vedutas, this is always and subtly ambiguous: "he lets it slip away, though maintaining the appearance of having respected it." The capriccio does not constitute the dark side, an inversion of the "real," though it is the momentary isolation of a constant procedure in his pictorial and graphic work. If his "objectivity" constitutes a *cliché* even more entrenched than that which existed prior to Brandi's study, the capricci would effectively have to be the product of eccentricity, explainable by the taste of Smith's clients, and would elude any investigation. But if this objectivity were less absolute, one would have to see his entire oeuvre in a new way, one which would be capable of encompassing *at the same time* the focus of his attention and his broad scope of his intervention into the imaginary. The two approaches are not contradictory, but complementary. The way in which Canaletto, in certain periods, worked simultaneously on vedutas and capricci indicates that they are not, for him, distinct genres, but two aspects of the same realm of experience: on the one hand the veduta, which concedes nothing but a reduced part to the imagination, in keeping with the bourgeois conception of the relationship between the individual and the world; on the other, the empirical study of the imaginary and its modes, its threshold of perceptibility, its effects, its transformation into vehicle. If the distinction between veduta and capriccio served to evaluate and compartmentalize his work, this is perhaps because Canal was one of the last painters to be able to master a domain which would later be divided in two. There is reason to believe that, from around 1750 on, the tendencies and aspirations that define any epoch are now manifested in single individuals, whereas up until then they were experienced together by every man and every artist as a sort of benevolent tension [...].

At the same time in which "everything is brought to the surface," this painting submits the veduta to a luminist alternative which justifies the liberties taken with perspective, and which tends to express light with colors not only liberated from grey, but as candid and austere as the rule of verisimilitude will allow; Canal disposes them, as Gioseffi aptly puts it, "in crisply inlaid fields." But why this sudden interest in light? Is he under the influence, as some say, of the *chiaristi* who took inspiration from the 16th century, like Sebastiano Ricci (1659–1743), Giovanni Antonio Pellegrini (1675–1741), Jacopo Amigoni (1682–1752) and Giambattista Pittoni (1687–1767)? If so, how does one explain their choice and, above all, why at the end of the 1720s? For an "influence" to take hold, there needs to be an interest on the part of the influenced—that is, the presence of a problem. Could it have been the *camera obscura*, which functioned well only in fine weather, that directed Canaletto's attention exclusively to moments of bright sunshine? A myopic explanation, like all those which rely on technological determinism.

The reason could have been more general and of livelier interest: the two principal features of the luminist painting which we have characterized seem in fact to have a common origin in the work of Newton. The philosopher died in 1727 and almost immediately the wheels which would take him, toward 1780, to near deification were set in motion. His *Opticks*, published in 1704, establishes modern color theory. The work scientifically describes, for the first time, their separation by a prism, an operation which separates light into its component colors which together produce "white light." It would not be absurd to sketch out a very general parallel between Newtonian theory and Canaletto's methods in the late 1720s [...]. If this regarded only the purification of color, then the coincidence would perhaps be merely fortuitous. But it concerns space as well. In 1686 Newton published *Philosophiae naturalis principia mathematica*, which opened with an extraordinarily shocking formula at the height of the baroque era: "absolute space, considered in its nature to be devoid of relation to anything extraneous, remains always homogeneous and immobile." This definition was a frontal challenge to the adherents of space-as-web, generated by bodies and elastically determined by them, since those same bodies set within Newton's space did not modify it at all [...] In its own way, Canaletto's painting of the 1720s

seems to possess these characteristics. The total transparency of the atmosphere creates the Newtonian void, in which buildings are immersed like distinct blocks, without any reciprocal interference and, at the same time, unscathed by contaminations from the surrounding air. These volumes do not seem to be on the verge of dissolving into smoke, as in Guardi: contained and coherent, they obey an ideal translated to perfection in the engravings of Visentini, whose strictly graphic means emphasize yet more forcefully the opposition of void and matter through the suppression of color. No matter how far away the gaze, every detail is offered in its full legibility: uniformity of representation, regardless of the distance from the observer. Uniformity also in the treatment of water, with the invention of an iterative brushstroke (inimitable in its deceptively "mechanical" quality).

Fixed movement: the boats leave no wake. Signification of objects by way of a repertoire of ever more synthetic signs; abstract manipulation of the relationships between bodies; even dissociation of these bodies, to which the painter adds or subtracts elements without undermining their identity (or, if one prefers, "identifiability"). The parallel we have sketched here raises several objections. We have chosen our epithets, moved the cursor all the way over to the "intellectual" position: to bring it back to "spontaneity," there are the opposing forces of the sensuality of brushwork, the poetic skies, that acidic morning light.

Certainly, and fortunately: we do not wish to reduce Canaletto to a mere scheme. But if we can avoid descending into vulgar determinism, we would be more than satisfied if the Newtonian nexus were seen as being plausible, even if it is an indirect Newtonism, in some ways refracted through numerous mediations.

(A. Corboz, *Canaletto. Una Venezia immaginaria*, 1985)

As protector of the arts and owner of a superb library, Smith enjoyed enormous fame in Venice, and was therefore in contact with nearly all of the most important artists. He was also an assiduous theatergoer and an opera enthusiast. His palazzo on the Canal Grande, near the church of the Apostoli, was the preferred meeting place of the nobles and intellectuals of the more audacious cut, for in addition to nourishing a great interest in erudite works and fine editions, Smith was always disposed to publish certain books which, in isolated Venice, would have appeared polemical if not outright subversive. Among his habitual guests was the sarcastic and anticonformist Padre Lodoli, who was usually accompanied by his vivacious student, the patrician Andrea Memmo. The new direction of Smith's patronage was signalled above all by the rapport with Canaletto, and in this regard it should be said that this rapport was fundamental for both of them. Though we cannot claim with certainty that they knew each other prior to 1729, Canaletto probably

began working for Smith one or two years before that, when he was already a well-known artist with a European clientele. Smith then began channeling almost all the painter's work toward England, from his own collection as well as from Canaletto's studio; despite the long-standing and vociferous arguments concerning the relations which united painter and patron, they remain still now mysterious. That which is certain is that the control exercised by Smith over Canaletto was such that most (if not all) the commissions entrusted to the artist passed through him. Things were not always easy, given the notoriously difficult personalities of both men: "and this is not the first time that I am forced to bow to the impertinence of a painter in order to best serve myself and my friends", wrote an angry Smith following a clash with Canaletto in 1729.
(F. Haskell, *Mecenati e pittori*, Florence 1985)

An ideal city, built with knowing deliberation. The first indications are seen in his sure-handed treatment of the material aspects, the disposition of buildings, etc. Though he was an acute observer of every aspect of Venice (as the drawings confirm), he discreetly asserts his artistic right to modify, transpose and reorganize these aspects in the interest of creating a painting. One of the first results of this process is the preservation, perhaps indeed the intensification, of the overall air of verisimilitude of the finished work.
Another, and more significant indication of Canaletto's exercise of a pure art is his treatment of the individual detail, particularly in the "wide-angle" perspectives of his mature period, where the eye of the viewer is treated to an enchanting, but literally impossible exultation of apparently infinite details, which in reality would require a telescope to be visible.
Canaletto always seems to promise, beyond appearance, other roofs, other doors half cast in shadow, and other windows, each with its stained glass panes. Only rarely does he entirely close off a composition. More often there is another corner to turn at the edge of the view, rendered seductive by a ray of sunlight, and the viewer identifies with the last, miniscule figure in the painting, destined to remain there forever, on the verge of disappearing into the shadowed cool of the surroundings.
(M. Levey, "Canaletto as Artist of the Urban Scene", in *Canaletto*, catalogue of the exhibition, 1989)

Essential Bibliography

C. Brandi, *Canaletto*, Milan 1960.

W.J. Constable, *Canaletto*, Oxford 1962.

I vedutisti veneziani del Settecento, exhibition catalogue, edited by P. Zampetti, Venice 1967.

G. Berto, L. Puppi, *L'opera completa del Canaletto*, Milan 1968.

G. Briganti, *I vedutisti*, Milan 1968.

J. Links, *Canaletto*, Oxford 1981.

Canaletto. Disegni dipinti incisioni, exhibition catalogue, edited by A. Bettagno, Venice 1982.

A. Corboz, *Canaletto. Una Venezia immaginaria*, Milan 1985.

F. Haskell, *Mecenati e pittori*, Florence 1985.

Canaletto, exhibition catalogue, edited by K. Baetjer and J. Links, New York, The Metropolitan Museum, 1989.

E. Mijnlieff, heading: "Canaletto/Giovanni Antonio Canal," in *La pittura in Italia. Il Settecento*, edited by G. Briganti, Milan 1990.